A Note From Denise Renner

The Word of God is so powerful in our lives. It is essential that every person spend time with God and study His Word in order to stay spiritually strong in these last days.

This study guide corresponds to my *TIME With Denise Renner* TV program by the same title that can be viewed at **deniserenner.org**. My desire is that through these lessons, you find the encouragement and freedom in Christ that you need. I believe the Holy Spirit is going to speak to you through the words you read in this study tool and that as you begin to use it, you will be *propelled* into the abundant life God has planned for you. I encourage you to make the effort to receive all He has for you and all He wants to do in you — it will definitely be worth it!

Whether you have walked with the Lord a long time or have just begun to follow Him, there is so much He wants to give you from His Word. He sees where you are, and He wants to meet you there.

> **Therefore do not worry about tomorrow, for tomorrow will worry about its own things. Sufficient for the day is its own trouble.**
> **Matthew 6:34**

Your sister and friend in Jesus Christ,

Denise Renner

Denise Renner

I0202201

Unless otherwise indicated, all scripture quotations are taken from the *New King James Version*®. Copyright © 1982 by Thomas Nelson. Used by permission. All rights reserved.

The Prize Is Waiting for You

Copyright © 2023 by Denise Renner
1814 W. Tacoma St.
Broken Arrow, Oklahoma 74012-1406

Published by Rick Renner Ministries
www.renner.org

ISBN 13: 978-1-6675-0319-6

eBook ISBN 13: 978-1-6675-0320-2

All rights reserved. No portion of this book may be reproduced or transmitted in any form or by any means — electronic, mechanical, photocopy, recording, scanning, or other (except for brief quotations in critical reviews or articles) — without the prior written permission of the Publisher.

TOPIC

There Is an Imperishable Crown Waiting for You

SCRIPTURES

1. **1 Corinthians 9:25** — And everyone who competes for the prize is temperate in all things. Now they do it to obtain a perishable crown, but we for an imperishable crown.

2. **Hebrews 12:1** — Therefore we also, since we are surrounded by so great a cloud of witnesses, let us lay aside every weight, and the sin which so easily ensnares us, and let us run with endurance the race that is set before us.

3. **Proverbs 16:32** — He who is slow to anger is better than the mighty, And he who rules his spirit than he who takes a city.

4. **Romans 8:28** — And we know that all things work together for good to those who love God, to those who are called according to His purpose.

5. **1 Samuel 25:24-26** — So she fell at his feet and said: "On me, my lord, on me let this iniquity be! And please let your maidservant speak in your ears, and hear the words of your maidservant. Please, let not my lord regard this scoundrel Nabal. For as his name is, so is he: Nabal is his name, and folly is with him! But I, your maidservant, did not see the young men of my lord whom you sent. Now therefore, my lord, as the Lord lives and as your soul lives, since the Lord has held you back from coming to bloodshed and from avenging yourself with your own hand, now then, let your enemies and those who seek harm for my lord be as Nabal."

6. **1 Samuel 25:31** — That this will be no grief to you, nor offense of heart to my lord, either that you have shed blood without cause, or that my lord has avenged himself. But when the Lord has dealt well with my lord, then remember your maidservant.

SYNOPSIS

Every believer has a spiritual race to run on this earth. If a believer has run his race well and finished his course, there waits for him an imperishable crown in heaven. While it's easy to become distracted or weighted down while running the race, the Bible teaches that believers must strip off the sin and the weight to run effectively. Endurance is key to finishing the race properly, and there is one Bible character in particular who demonstrates what true commitment and endurance really look like. An overview of the Old Testament hero Abigail provides insight into how a believer can remain committed during the difficult times and eventually win the race!

The emphasis of this lesson:

There was a great woman in David's time named Abigail who demonstrated powerful commitment, endurance, humility, wisdom, and boldness. Although she was placed in a difficult position, Abigail chose not to become the victim but rather the victor. Her commitment to her marriage and to God eventually saved her entire household from certain death at the hands of David and his army. Her boldness and godly character will encourage you to remain committed to your race even in the face of challenging situations!

The Imperishable Crown

If you're a believer, you have a race of faith to run for the Kingdom of God. Like all natural races, your spiritual race has a prize you can win in the end. This is why the Bible admonishes believers to pay attention to how they run their race so they can reach the finish line and obtain the prize that awaits them.

The prize for completing your spiritual race far exceeds any natural trophy or medal. Those things will only last for a certain time and will eventually rust, fade, or break. God's rewards are eternal and never pass away. First Corinthians 9:25 says, "And everyone who competes for the prize is temperate in all things. Now they do it to obtain a perishable crown, but we for an imperishable crown." The crown we can receive at the end of our race is imperishable and incorruptible. It will last for all eternity! Knowing the immeasurable value of our prize makes it worth pushing through any difficulty we have here on earth in order to receive our crown!

There will come a day when Jesus congratulates the winners of this race. If you've been obedient to His plan and ran your race well, He will say to you, "Well done, thou good and faithful servant" (*see* Matthew 25:21). He will then place that imperishable winner's crown on your head! You will wear it for all eternity as the prize for finishing your spiritual race on earth.

Running the Race

For many Christians, the reality of running an eternal race isn't something they think about often. However, the Bible teaches that each one of us is responsible to run our race properly and in accordance with God's plan. In expounding on our race, Hebrews 12:1 says, "Therefore we also, since we are surrounded by so great a cloud of witnesses, let us lay aside every weight, and the sin which so easily ensnares us, and let us run with endurance the race that is set before us."

As we run our race, we are being observed by others who have gone on to Heaven before us. They are what Hebrews 12 refers to as the "great cloud of witnesses." As we progress in our spiritual race, they are cheering us on from the grandstands of Heaven.

If you've had a loved one who was a believer in your life who's already gone home to Heaven, you can rest assured they are watching you run your race here on earth. Perhaps it's a family member, a friend, a pastor, or a Sunday School teacher, whomever you loved here on earth and was part of the family of God is cheering you from the balcony of Heaven as you make strides in the spirit. That great cloud of witnesses is watching you! They've already entered the Kingdom of Heaven and know the glory that is waiting for you if you'll run and finish your race. They're cheering you on to continue in your race and press through any difficulty, discouragement, or setback. They are rooting for you to win the prize!

Another thing we need to realize as we run our race is how weight and sin can hinder us. Hebrews 12:1 admonishes us to "lay aside every weight, and the sin which so easily ensnares us." If we don't strip off these things, we may not reach the finish line and ultimately would have to forfeit our crown.

In Roman times, serious runners were required to strip off almost all their clothes so they could run swiftly and deftly. Nothing hindered them as they remained focused on their goal of winning the race. Similarly, we have to get rid of anything that can trip us up in our spiritual race. We have to repent of sin, release forgiveness, and remove any distractions. We can't run encumbered by unnecessary weights and sins that would hinder us from reaching the finish line.

Finally, we have to run with endurance. This means that sometimes the race may get difficult or cumbersome. However, if we want to run to win, we must endure even the most challenging seasons of faith and obedience as we follow God's plan. If we faint or lose heart during the hard times, we can get knocked out of the race and lose the prize God has for us!

Abigail's Example of Endurance

A great example in the Bible of someone who endured her race in the hard times was a woman in the Old Testament named Abigail. Although she was placed in a very difficult situation, she acted with wisdom and grace. Her brave actions ultimately saved her family, making her a hero in the Bible.

Abigail's story takes place in First Samuel 25. She was married to a wealthy man named Nabal who owned quite a bit of land, and thousands of sheep and goats. Unfortunately, Nabal also had some real character issues. He was hard, cruel, stiff-necked, stubborn, obstinate, hard-hearted, and impatient. In fact, the Bible calls him a scoundrel!

You can imagine how difficult it would be to be married to someone like this. However, Abigail remained committed to her marriage, even though Nabal was not an easy person to get along with. That commitment was part of the race she had to run. It was a difficult thing to endure, but she held fast to her promise and stayed committed.

Commitment is a powerful quality that's required as we run our race. We might find ourselves in difficult situations, but if we will remain committed to the race God has set in front of us, that commitment will pay off in the end.

Even during Jesus' earthly ministry, He was looking for commitment from His disciples. He once asked Peter, "Are you going to leave me too?" Peter replied, "Lord, where could we go? You're the only one with the words of eternal life" (*see* John 6:67-69).

Peter's view on commitment is one we need to adopt as well in *our* Christian walk. Jesus is the only one with the words of eternal life. How can we not stay committed when Jesus is our Life Source?

In Abigail's case, she had made a commitment to stay in her marriage and remain faithful to God. It wasn't an easy place for her, but she was a woman who was determined to do what was right in the sight of God. Her ability to endure eventually was rewarded in the end.

One day, King David and his men came into Abigail's village. Through a series of events, David and his men wound up protecting Nabal's sheep from nearby thieves. Later, they asked Nabal to return the favor by providing them some food during a feast day. To their astonishment, Nabal refused to help them! This belligerent action infuriated David so much that he decided to send his men into Nabal's home and fields to wipe out his entire household.

Before David could carry out his retaliation, Abigail ran to meet him and interceded on Nabal's behalf. Because Abigail had a different attitude about her — a committed heart to her marriage and to God — she didn't see herself as a victim. She was a victor!

The Bible tells us that "He who is slow to anger is better than the mighty, And he who rules his spirit than he who takes a city" (Proverbs 16:32). Abigail is a good example of someone who applied this scripture in her daily life. Although her circumstances were difficult and she was treated unjustly by her husband and his actions, she didn't let anger rule her. Because she was committed to godly character, when presented with the opportunity to embrace anger, she refused. She controlled her anger, submitted to God, and allowed God to do something inside her.

When Abigail first heard that David was coming to carry out his vengeance upon Nabal, she gathered up an ample supply of food to give to David and his men. The Bible says her offering included 200 loaves of bread, wine, 5 sheep, roasted grain, 100 clusters of raisins, and 200 fig cakes. She then loaded these gifts on donkeys and headed straight toward David's army.

In this life-threatening situation, Abigail had an incredible amount of wisdom. She knew exactly what to do to bring peace to the situation. She wasn't angry or playing the role of a victim; rather, she acted in great wisdom and humility.

When Abigail finally reached David and his men, she fell at his feet and cried, "On me, my lord, on me let this iniquity be! And please let your maidservant speak in your ears, and hear the words of your maidservant. Please, let not my lord regard this scoundrel Nabal. For as his name is, so is he: Nabal is his name, and folly is with him! But I, your maidservant, did not see the young men of my lord whom you sent. Now therefore, my lord, as the Lord lives and as your soul lives, since the Lord has held you back from coming to bloodshed and from avenging yourself with your own hand, now then, let your enemies and those who seek harm for my lord be as Nabal" (1 Samuel 25:24-26).

In essence, Abigail was pleading for the blame to be placed on her even though it was Nabal who was responsible for this conundrum. She humbled herself as she interceded on behalf of her husband. Out of her commitment came great humility, and out of that humility came great power and boldness to stand before David and negotiate with him.

Recognizing that David's intended actions would be just as disastrous for him and his future, Abigail pleaded with David, "That this will be no grief to you, nor offense of heart to my lord, either that you have shed blood without cause, or that my lord has avenged himself. But when the Lord has dealt well with my lord, then remember your maidservant" (1 Samuel 25:31). Her words demonstrated a great depth of wisdom and boldness!

Abigail was able to pull out of her spirit a reservoir of boldness because she was a woman of humility, commitment, and endurance. Her character not only saved her own life, but it also spared her husband's life and salvaged David's reputation. Because of her commitment, blood was not shed that day!

Friends, we can learn so much from Abigail's example. If fear is trying to push you around or if there is a person endeavoring to intimidate you, don't cower down. Instead, remember Abigail and stay the course. Be committed. Remain humble. Don't be the victim, but see yourself as the victor! Let God's wisdom and boldness rise up on the inside of you. He has a rescue plan for your situation!

The Lord will give you boldness to stand up for what's right. You don't have to listen to the opinions of others or the accusations of the enemy. You can remain humble before God and stand up against any enemy that comes your way.

Don't Be Knocked Out of the Race

As you run your race, you may encounter a variety of situations, people, or events that could try to hinder you from completing your course. However, it's important for you to stay committed and keep your eyes on the finish line. Don't let anything or anyone knock you out of the race God has set before you.

Romans 8:28 is an important reminder: "And we know that all things work together for good to those who love God, to those who are called according to His purpose." We can trust God that He is working things out for our good. Even when we run into challenges and difficulties, if we will remain committed to the race, God will work out things on our behalf.

By running our race with endurance, we can make it to the end and eventually win the prize set before us. When we stand before Jesus, we can hear Him say, "Well done, thou good and faithful servant." Then He will present us with our prize — the unperishable crown that will never fade away.

STUDY QUESTIONS

Be diligent to present yourself approved to God, a worker who does not need to be ashamed, rightly dividing the word of truth.
— 2 Timothy 2:15

1. First Corinthians 9:25 says, "And everyone who competes for the prize is temperate in all things. Now they do it to obtain a perishable crown, but we for an imperishable crown." How often do you think about the crown laid up for you in Heaven? If you approached your life with that eternal perspective, how would it change your attitudes, actions, and behaviors?

2. Hebrews 12:1 reminds us that we are surrounded by a great cloud of witnesses. Who do you have in that cloud that is cheering you on? A parent or grandparent? A teacher, a pastor, a friend?

3. Romans 8:28 says, "And we know that all things work together for good to those who love God, to those who are called according to His purpose." Can you recall a difficult time you experienced that God worked out for your good and for His purpose?

PRACTICAL APPLICATION

But be doers of the word,
and not hearers only, deceiving yourselves.
—James 1:22

Cultivate commitment as you run your race.

1. If you were in Abigail's shoes, how would you have responded to Nabal or to David's vengeance? How does her story inspire you to cultivate commitment in your life?

2. How are you running the race God has called you to run? What weights and sins are hanging onto you that you need to remove?

3. Has someone or something ever tried to discourage you from running your race? Did you give in to the discouragement, or did you stand up in boldness and continue pressing onward to the finish line?

LESSON 2

TOPIC

Don't Quit — The Prize Is Worth It

SCRIPTURES

1. **1 Corinthians 9:24** — Do you not know that those who run in a race all run, but one receives the prize? Run in such a way that you may obtain it.

2. **Hebrews 12:1** — Therefore we also, since we are surrounded by so great a cloud of witnesses, let us lay aside every weight, and the sin which so easily ensnares us, and let us run with endurance the race that is set before us.

3. **Esther 4:14-16** — For if you remain completely silent at this time, relief and deliverance will arise for the Jews from another place, but you and your father's house will perish. Yet who knows whether you have come to the kingdom for such a time as this? Then Esther told them to reply to Mordecai: "Go gather all the Jews who are present in Shushan, and fast for me; neither eat nor drink for three days, night

or day. My maids and I will fast likewise. And so I will go to the king, which is against the law; and if I perish, I perish!"

4. **Esther 5:2-4** — So it was, when the king saw Queen Esther standing in the court, that she found favor in his sight, and the king held out to Esther the golden scepter that was in his hand. Then Esther went near and touched the top of the scepter. And the king said to her, "What do you wish, Queen Esther? What is your request? It shall be given to you — up to half the kingdom! So Esther answered, "If it pleases the king, let the king and Haman come today to the banquet that I have prepared for him."

SYNOPSIS

Esther is a powerful example in the Bible of someone who ran her race well — even in the face of extreme danger and possible death. Because she chose to humble herself before God and receive His detailed plan, the Lord navigated her to safety in an impossible situation. As she learned to endure the difficult part of her race, God used her position to save a nation!

The emphasis of this lesson:

In order to win the prize for your spiritual race, you must learn to cultivate endurance in your life. One aspect of endurance is listening for God's details and obeying Him carefully in everything He instructs you to do. While those details may seem unimportant at the time, you can rest assured that God is weaving together an intricate picture of His plan for you. As you submit to Him and follow His instructions, He'll lead you step by step into His perfect plan for your life.

You Have a Race To Run

As we saw in the last lesson, every believer has a spiritual race to run on earth. In First Corinthians 9:24, Paul asked the question, "Do you not know that those who run in a race all run, but one receives the prize?" He then admonished, "Run in such a way that you may obtain it."

In our Christian walk, we have to strip off weights and sins and run our race with endurance so that we may win the imperishable crown that awaits us in Heaven. We are running with a specific goal in mind, and that is to hear Jesus say, "Well done, thou good and faithful servant" (*see* Matthew 25:21). If we complete our race properly, Jesus will one day present us with our eternal reward.

The Bible tells us that while we are running our race here on earth, those saints who have passed on to Glory are now watching us from Heaven (*see* Hebrews 12:1). This great cloud of witnesses is cheering us on to the finish line. Even the saints of old — like Abraham, King David, and the apostle Paul — are part of this wonderful cast observing us from the grandstands of Heaven. Believers we knew in this life who have gone home to Heaven are also sitting in this wonderful cheering squad. As they peer over the balcony of Heaven and note our progress in the spirit, they are all shouting, "Go! Go! You can make it! You can run and finish the race! You can win the prize!"

Esther's Example of Endurance

Any athletic competition requires a certain amount of endurance to be able to stay in the game and win the trophy. Our spiritual life is no different. As we run the race God has set before us, it's necessary that we develop the endurance and tenacity to stick with our assignment even in the midst of difficult situations. This endurance is critical to overcoming the hurdles and pressing through to victory.

One powerful example in the Old Testament of someone who ran her race with endurance is Queen Esther. The book of Esther chronicles the story of how this remarkable young Jewish woman — who was orphaned and raised by her uncle Mordecai — ended up becoming queen during Israel's captivity. While her origins made her an unlikely candidate to save a nation, God used her to preserve her people in a very dangerous time. Because Esther chose to endure through the difficulty and run her race to the finish line, she became a hero in the Bible. She is certainly one of the spectators who is watching us from the grandstands of Heaven and cheering us on in our race!

Esther's story begins during an intense period in Israel's history. At the time, the Jews were an occupied people, and the Persian king, Ahasuerus, ruled over them. One day, the king threw a royal banquet, but his wife, Queen Vashti, refused to attend. This act of defiance infuriated the king, and he immediately dethroned her and had her removed from his palace.

In search of a new bride, the king sent out a decree for all the young virgins in the empire to be gathered up and taken to the palace. There, they would undergo beauty treatments for several months and then be presented to the king. He would choose one of them to be his wife, and the rest would be counted among the king's concubines.

Esther was one of the young virgins who was captured and brought to the palace. She was forced to leave her home, her family, and the life she knew. However, God had a powerful plan for Esther, and she willingly let herself be used for His purposes! During her beauty treatments, Esther found great favor with her captors and ultimately became the woman King Ahasuerus chose as his queen. Little did she know, God had sovereignly placed her in that position for His plan.

One day during Esther's reign as queen, her uncle Mordecai came to her with a sobering situation. The king's most powerful appointed leader, Haman — Mordecai's enemy and the enemy of the Jewish people — was hatching a plot to kill all the Jews in the empire. The only way to stop the plan was for Esther to intervene on the Jews' behalf and plead her case before the king.

When Mordecai presented this grave problem to her, Esther realized the risk she would have to take to approach the king without the king's request — an action that was punishable by death. However, Mordecai warned Esther of what would happen if she didn't use her position to save her people: "For if you remain completely silent at this time, relief and deliverance will arise for the Jews from another place, but you and your father's house will perish. Yet who knows whether you have come to the kingdom for such a time as this?" (Esther 4:14).

Understanding that she would need God to guide her through this critical crossroads, Esther replied to Mordecai, "Go gather all the Jews who are present in Shushan, and fast for me; neither eat nor drink for three days, night or day. My maids and I will fast likewise. And so I will go to the king, which is against the law; and if I perish, I perish!" (Esther 4:16).

During Esther's fast, God gave her a brilliant plan. He filled her with great wisdom and boldness, and then He awarded her favor with the king. When she approached the king uninvited, he received her graciously. Her request to him was simple: To host the king and Haman for a banquet at the palace. Intrigued by this request, the king accepted her dinner invitation.

The night of the banquet, Esther posed another request: To host a second banquet for the king and Haman. They both readily agreed to come to another dinner party. All throughout this process, God was giving Esther wisdom in the details. He knew just how to soften the king's heart, and He was protecting Esther in her assignment.

At the second banquet, Esther broached the subject of Haman's plan to exterminate the Jews. Because of God's wisdom, she was able to expose Haman right in front of the king. In the end, the king ordered Haman to be punished and for Esther's people to be spared from annihilation.

What a powerful conclusion for Esther's bravery and humility! Although she was placed in an impossible situation, she endured until the end. She fasted, prayed, and waited upon the Lord for instruction and direction. When God gave her a plan, she obeyed. She listened to every detail and carried them out fully. As a result, she was able to fulfill her assignment and run her race well!

Listen to the Details

Another valuable takeaway from Esther's story is the importance of listening to the details God gives us in executing His plan. Sometimes it's easy to overlook the details because they seem so unimportant. But if God gives us specific steps in His plan, it's extremely important we pay close attention to the details and follow through with them just as He said. God's plan is so intricate and requires our cooperation, even in the little things He shows us.

In explaining the necessity of listening for God's details, Denise shared a story of how she missed some of the details of God's plan for her in her early years and how the Lord mercifully led her back into the place she was supposed to be. Denise recalled that when she was a young woman, she originally enrolled in a college she knew wasn't the one she was to attend. She ended up crying herself to sleep every night because she had no peace in her heart about her school. Although the Lord was blessing her singing and her education, she felt miserable.

One day, the Lord spoke to Denise through another individual: "If you stay here in this school that I didn't tell you to go to, I'll bless you. But you'll never know what it was I wanted to show you." After that warning, Denise found herself in an impossible situation. Her tuition was already paid for at her current school, and she didn't have the money to attend the other school. However, she decided to obey God and trust Him to provide the necessary funds for her education.

Soon, God performed a miracle for Denise and provided the money she needed for the other school. After transferring over to the new university, she knew the Lord was speaking to her to take voice lessons from a certain instructor. Although she wanted a different teacher, she submitted to the leading of the Holy Spirit. The Lord even worked out her schedule so she could be in this professor's class!

Denise recognized that God was working out even the smallest details as He navigated her back into His will for her life. Step by step, He was leading her in her education. As a reward for her obedience, she eventually met a young man at this college by the name of Rick Renner. Because Denise paid attention to God's details and repented when she missed His way, the Lord led her to her future husband!

Being in the right place at the right time is critical to walking in God's plan and running our race properly. God is in the details, and if we'll listen to Him carefully, He'll show us exactly what to do, when to do it, who to be with, and where to be. Listening to God's details and executing them correctly even when we don't understand or don't like what God is telling us is all part of running our race with endurance. By submitting to God's details, we'll eventually find ourselves right in the middle of God's plan!

Think about all the people who listened to the Lord on September 11, 2001. Many people heard the Lord warn them not to go to work that day, not to go in a certain direction, or not to take their child to lunch at a particular place. The detail seemed so insignificant at the time, but it later proved to be an invaluable leading as God was protecting His children from danger and death.

The Bible admonishes us to be aware of the dangerous times we live in before Jesus' return. We need to be strong in these last days and pay attention to the details the Lord shows us. It's imperative we listen to the Holy Spirit and obey what He speaks to our hearts. He will get us through impossible situations as we run our race.

To endure until the end, we must listen and obey. We can follow Esther's example in enduring until the end. By humbling ourselves before the Lord and listening to His detailed plan, we can boldly carry out our divine assignments here on earth. Our race has a finish line, and we can run to win the prize!

STUDY QUESTIONS

Be diligent to present yourself approved to God, a worker
who does not need to be ashamed, rightly dividing the word of truth.
— 2 Timothy 2:15

1. First Corinthians 9:24 says, "Do you not know that those who run in a race all run, but one receives the prize? Run in such a way that you may obtain it." Have you been running your race in such a way as to obtain the prize waiting for you? If not, what do you need to change?

2. Esther 4 reveals the great risk Esther had to take in order to obey God fully and fulfill her assignment. What risks has God asked you to take as you follow His plan for your life?

3. Esther 5 tells the story of the wise plan God gave Esther in a time of great danger. Can you think of a time in your life when you were faced with an impossible situation, and God gave you the necessary wisdom and instruction to navigate safely through the difficulty?

PRACTICAL APPLICATION

But be doers of the word,
and not hearers only, deceiving yourselves.
— James 1:22

Learn to listen to God's details.

1. Take a moment to reflect on God's details in your life. What was one detail He gave you that seemed insignificant at the time but proved to be key to your assignment?

2. When has the Lord prompted you *not* to do something and that detail ended up being important for your safety?

3. What impossible situations have you been in recently where you've had to learn to endure in order to finish your race?

TOPIC

Endurance Is Working Out Its Power in You

SCRIPTURES

1. **Daniel 1:8** — But Daniel purposed in his heart that he would not defile himself with the portion of the king's delicacies, nor with the wine which he drank; therefore he requested of the chief of the eunuchs that he might not defile himself.

2. **James 4:10** — Humble yourselves in the sight of the Lord, and He will lift you up.

3. **Daniel 2:27,28** — Daniel answered in the presence of the king, and said, "The secret which the king has demanded, the wise men, the astrologers, the magicians, and the soothsayers cannot declare to the king. But there is a God in heaven who reveals secrets, and He has made known to King Nebuchadnezzar what will be in the latter days…."

4. **Deuteronomy 29:29** — The secret things belong to the Lord our God, but those things which are revealed belong to us and to our children forever, that we may do all the words of this law.

5. **John 14:26** — But the Helper, the Holy Spirit, whom the Father will send in My name, He will teach you all things, and bring to your remembrance all things that I said to you.

SYNOPSIS

Daniel is an inspiring example of how to run the race of faith in the midst of difficult and dangerous times. Taken as a political prisoner by the Babylonians, Daniel had every opportunity to become bitter at his captors and his circumstances. But instead of choosing the path of unforgiveness, he remained committed to God, His commands, and His character. As a result of this level of commitment, God positioned Daniel in the Babylonian kingdom to declare the truth of His eternal Kingdom to a very wicked king!

The emphasis of this lesson:

Running the race of faith requires us to strip off the weights and sins that can easily distract us. As we learn from Daniel's example of commitment, forgiveness is a critical key to running our race effectively. We also need to tap into the supernatural wisdom of God through the power of the Holy Spirit. God will reveal great secrets to us if we'll listen to Him, and those secrets will help us finish our race and win the prize.

Your Race Is Serious!

As we've seen in the last few lessons, the Bible teaches that we have a spiritual race to run on this earth. This race has an eternal prize waiting for us at the finish line — an imperishable crown that will never fade away. To receive this crown, we have to press in with all our might to the end of the race. This requires us to stay focused on the goal as we run with endurance the race God has set before us.

Our race isn't something to be taken lightly, and the rewards of finishing well aren't something we'll shove in the closet and forget about. It's a very serious race we're running with eternal consequences! As the time of Jesus' return draws nearer, the days we live in will continue to become more dangerous and difficult. We'll have to keep our eyes focused on Jesus at all times in order to reach the finish line and win our prize. This race requires our absolute and complete commitment if we want to hear Jesus say to us, "Well done, thou good and faithful servant!"

Daniel's Example of Commitment

One person in the Old Testament who demonstrated commitment as he ran his spiritual race was Daniel. He was truly an extraordinary person who endured some very difficult circumstances and still remained faithful to God. Daniel ran his race well and certainly won the prize that was waiting for him in eternity!

Daniel's story takes place during a challenging period in Israel's history when the nation was occupied by foreign kingdoms. As a young man, Daniel was taken captive along with several of his friends and was made to serve in the palace of the Babylonian king, Nebuchadnezzar. He was forced to become a eunuch and had to integrate into the culture and customs of the Babylonians. He lost his language, his Jewish culture, and his name.

As you can imagine, this was not an easy time for Daniel, but he didn't let the challenges in life pull him down. Instead, he stayed focused on his race. He pressed through the hard times and allowed God to use him — even in captivity.

The primary quality that set Daniel apart is found in Daniel 1:8, "But Daniel purposed in his heart that he would not defile himself with the portion of the king's delicacies, nor with the wine which he drank; therefore he requested of the chief of the eunuchs that he might not defile himself." The phrase "purposed in his heart" reveals Daniel's level of commitment to the Lord. He determined in his heart that he would not eat or drink things that were contrary to God's commands. This was an inner consecration to God that was demonstrated outwardly in Daniel's actions.

As a result of Daniel's consecration, he found favor in the sight of the king and his captors. In fact, the Bible tells us that Daniel and his friends increased in knowledge and wisdom so much that they were found to be ten times wiser than the great magicians in the king's court! It wasn't easy for Daniel and his fellow Jewish friends to stand strong in their commitment to the Lord. It took great courage for them to boldly stand up for God in the midst of a pagan society.

Later in Daniel's story, King Nebuchadnezzar had a disturbing dream. He searched for anyone in the kingdom who could interpret his dream and ended up threatening to kill all the wise men in his court who failed to do so. Filled with the boldness and wisdom of God, Daniel confronted the king and was able to interpret the dream correctly.

Daniel 2:27,28 says, "Daniel answered in the presence of the king, and said, 'The secret which the king has demanded, the wise men, the astrologers, the magicians, and the soothsayers cannot declare to the king. But there is a God in heaven who reveals secrets, and He has made known to King Nebuchadnezzar what will be in the latter days....'"

Although Daniel was mistreated and taken captive against his will as a young man, he chose to keep the right heart and forgive his political enemies. He remained committed to his faith in a difficult and dangerous time. As a result, God gave him supernatural wisdom and boldness, revealing secrets to him that no one else could understand.

Daniel's commitment to the race set him on a course to be positioned by God for His purposes — even in a godless environment. Equipped with wisdom, favor, and supernatural revelation, he was God's person to come on the scene at just the right moment. This divine setup opened up the way for Daniel to declare the truth about God and His eternal kingdom to Nebuchadnezzar, the most powerful and wicked king of the time.

Keep Running Your Race

Daniel's story teaches us a very important lesson about the power of forgiveness and how it can help us finish our race properly. As a young man, Daniel was treated terribly by those in power. All through his life, he — along with the rest of the Israelites — was basically held as a political prisoner in the Babylonian kingdom. This type of upbringing and catastrophe could have made Daniel an extremely bitter person. However, instead of choosing to let anger and bitterness take root in his heart, he chose to forgive his enemies. That forgiveness was key to moving forward in God's plan for his life.

Unforgiveness is one of those powerful heart attitudes that can hinder us from running our race. It's a sin and a heavy weight that can easily trip us up and get us off course. If we don't learn to strip off unforgiveness and let go of hurt, anger, or bitterness, we won't reach the finish line. Unforgiveness can literally interrupt our race!

Daniel's story also shows us how valuable God's wisdom can be in our life. Deuteronomy 29:29 says, "The secret things belong to the Lord our God, but those things which are revealed belong to us and to our children forever, that we may do all the words of this law." There are secret things that only God knows! By tapping into his wisdom, He will reveal to us secret things that will help us do His will.

God wants to reveal Himself to us, and that includes the secret things pertaining to His plan. Through the Person of the Holy Spirit, God guides us into all truth. John 14:26 says, "But the Helper, the Holy Spirit, whom the Father will send in My name, He will teach you all things, and bring to your remembrance all things that I said to you." The Holy Spirit will bring scripture to our hearts, revealing the truth of God's Word to us. He will show us things to come and reveal the mysteries and secrets of God's plan. He's our helper, and He was sent to help us run and finish our race.

As we run the race God has set before us, let's remember to strip off all the weights and sins that can so easily entangle us and pull us off track. Like Daniel, we can choose to forgive others even when we've been mistreated or marginalized. If we'll allow God's love to rule and reign in our hearts, we can run our race free from the chains of anger and bitterness. Our commitment to God can open up God's wisdom to us, and we can know "secret things" by revelation of the Holy Spirit. We can walk in the truth of God's eternal plan, run our race well, make it to the finish line, and win the eternal prize laid up for us in eternity!

STUDY QUESTIONS

Be diligent to present yourself approved to God, a worker
who does not need to be ashamed, rightly dividing the word of truth.
— 2 Timothy 2:15

1. Daniel 1:8 says, "But Daniel purposed in his heart that he would not defile himself with the portion of the king's delicacies, nor with the wine which he drank; therefore he requested of the chief of the eunuchs that he might not defile himself." How have you purposed in your heart to remain committed to God's Word and His plan?

2. Deuteronomy 29:29 says, "The secret things belong to the Lord our God, but those things which are revealed belong to us and to our children forever, that we may do all the words of this law." What secret things has God revealed to you that have helped you run your race?

3. John 14:26 says, "But the Helper, the Holy Spirit, whom the Father will send in My name, He will teach you all things, and bring to your remembrance all things that I said to you." Can you think of one time in particular when the Holy Spirit brought something back to your remembrance?

PRACTICAL APPLICATION

But be doers of the word,
and not hearers only, deceiving yourselves.
— James 1:22

Learn to run your race with forgiveness and wisdom!

1. If you were taken captive like Daniel, how would you have responded to your captors? Would you have trouble forgiving those who mistreated you?

2. Because Daniel and his friends purposed in their hearts to stay committed to God's commands, God gave them so much wisdom and understanding that they were ten times smarter than all the magicians and astrologers in the king's realm. Can you think of a time when you remained committed to God, and He filled you with wisdom — so much wisdom that you had more insight and understanding than your peers, colleagues, or classmates?

3. Daniel recognized that God knew secrets beyond man's understanding. What secrets has God revealed to you as you've walked with Him?

LESSON 4

TOPIC

Whatever It Takes, It Will Be Completely Worth It

SCRIPTURES

1. **Hebrews 12:1** — Therefore we also, since we are surrounded by so great a cloud of witnesses, let us lay aside every weight, and the sin which so easily ensnares us, and let us run with endurance the race that is set before us.

2. **2 Kings 4:30** — And the mother of the child said, "As the Lord lives, and as your soul lives, I will not leave you." So he arose and followed her.

SYNOPSIS

The Shunammite woman in Second Kings 4 is another wonderful example of what it means to run the race with great faith, boldness, and endurance. Although the catastrophe of the death of her son came into this woman's life, she decided to plan a resurrection instead of a funeral! As a result of her commitment and tenacity, the Shunammite woman received her promise…and a miracle!

The emphasis of this lesson:

As we run our spiritual race, we have to determine to let nothing push us out of the race. Taking our cues from the Shunammite woman in the Old Testament, we can learn to cultivate endurance, faith, and boldness as we approach the finish line. Jesus has a prize for us at the end of the race, and if we don't give up during difficult times, we can receive this glorious prize for all eternity!

Running To Win an Imperishable Crown

Scripture teaches us that we all have a prize waiting for us at the end of our spiritual race. Unlike trophies, medals, ribbons, or plaques that we win in natural races, our spiritual prize is something that won't fade away with time. It's an eternal reward — an imperishable crown — that Jesus will place on our heads when we get to Heaven. If we've run our race well here on earth, we will win the prize and hear Him say to us, "Well done, good and faithful servant" (*see* Matthew 25:21).

Each one of us has a very specific race that God has set before us. Your race will be different from the race your parents or your friends are called to run. God has a special race custom-made for you, and if you make it to the finish line of your race, Jesus has an imperishable crown just for you.

The Shunammite Woman's Example of Endurance

In Second Kings 4, there is a lesser-known story of a woman who had mighty faith to endure her race here on earth. Her name is not mentioned in the scriptures, but we know her as "the Shunammite woman." Although she was faced with a devastating hurdle at a certain point in her life, she remained full of faith and had the boldness to push through the difficulty to see her victory!

The Shunammite woman was a notable woman who lived during the time of Elisha the prophet. She was married to an older man and was never able to have children, but she chose to get as close to God as she could. Since the prophet was the only one who spoke for the Lord in the days of the Old Testament, this woman did what she could to take care of Elisha the prophet in support of his ministry and her hunger for God. She built a room for him in her house and offered him food and lodging.

One day, Elisha asked the Shunammite woman what he could do for her since she had been such a tremendous blessing to his life and ministry. Her deepest desire was to have a child because she was not able to conceive. In response to her need, Elisha prophesied to her that she and her husband would bear a child in one year!

As prophesied, the Shunammite woman miraculously bore a son within the next 12 months. But when the boy was a little older, he suddenly became gravely ill and died. Surprisingly, instead of mourning and grieving over her son's death, this woman mustered up great boldness and faith and began to plan his resurrection!

She chased down the prophet and pleaded with him to pray for her son. She was so tenacious in her request that she told Elisha, "As the Lord lives, and as your soul lives, I will not leave you" (*see* 2 Kings 2:2). She refused to leave the prophet alone until she got her miracle!

Finally, Elisha conceded to her plea and followed her home to pray for the young boy. In just a moment of time, life was brought back into the boy's body, and he was raised from the dead by the power of God. Because she was unwilling to let her promise be stolen from her, the Shunammite woman stayed in the race of faith until God supernaturally delivered her answer.

Don't Be Pushed Out of the Race

The extreme faith, boldness, and tenacity the Shunammite woman displayed is a wonderful example of what it takes to stay in the game. In order to finish our race and receive the promises of God, we have to cultivate that same type of commitment this woman had. We can't let the enemy steal God's promises from us, and we must push anything that's hindering us out of the way.

It takes boldness to rise up from potential defeat, and it requires courage to persevere until a miracle breaks through for us. We have to stay committed to God's Word and see any challenges through the eyes of faith. This is part of running our race with endurance — no matter what difficulties, setbacks, or problems arise, we have to determine in our hearts to press forward to the finish line.

Certain attitudes like unforgiveness or pride can easily creep into our lives and attempt to knock us off course. However, we must recognize the enemy's tactics and refuse to give in to those temptations. We have to allow the love of God to take root in our hearts and release forgiveness to others. When we're tempted to think more highly of ourselves than we ought, we can come boldly before God's throne and repent of our pride. He can easily change our character if we will let Him.

Regardless of what circumstances may be surrounding our children or family members, we can rise up in boldness and push the enemy away in Jesus' name. We can declare our children's future according to what the Word of God says about their future. If we will remain committed to our race and push through the difficulties, nothing can stand in our way as we press toward our prize.

There is a day coming when we will see Jesus face to face in heaven. If we've finished our race well, He will say to us, "Well done, thou good and faithful servant." He will then place that beautiful, imperishable crown upon our heads. At that moment, we will know that whatever price we had to pay in order to be faithful to the end was worth it.

STUDY QUESTIONS

Be diligent to present yourself approved to God, a worker who does not need to be ashamed, rightly dividing the word of truth.
— 2 Timothy 2:15

1. Hebrews 12:1 says, "Therefore we also, since we are surrounded by so great a cloud of witnesses, let us lay aside every weight, and the sin which so easily ensnares us, and let us run with endurance the race that is set before us." What weights have been trying to entangle you in your race recently? What are you doing to strip off those weights so you can finish your race?
2. When the Shunammite woman's son died, she planned a resurrection instead of a funeral. This demonstrated her great faith in God's promises! Have you ever had a promise "die" in your life, and you had to press through in faith to see its resurrection?
3. When the Shunammite woman approached Elisha and pleaded with him to come and pray for her son, she wasn't willing to take *no* for an answer. She told the prophet, "As the Lord lives, and as your soul lives, I will not leave you" (*see* 2 Kings 2:2). Can you think of a time when

you've had to demonstrate such tenacity and boldness in obtaining a promise from God?

PRACTICAL APPLICATION

**But be doers of the word,
and not hearers only, deceiving yourselves.**
—James 1:22

Don't let the enemy push you out of your race!

1. What promises from God have you received? How have you had to hold on to those promises in faith?

2. What enemies have tried to take your promise away from you? What did you do to push those enemies away so you could continue running your race?

3. What are some of your faith declarations for your children, your marriage, and your family?

TOPIC

Peace Is Waiting for You

SCRIPTURES

1. **Luke 10:38-42** — Now it happened as they went that He entered a certain village; and a certain woman named Martha welcomed Him into her house. And she had a sister called Mary, who also sat at Jesus' feet and heard His word. But Martha was distracted with much serving, and she approached Him and said, "Lord, do You not care that my sister has left me to serve alone? Therefore tell her to help me." And Jesus answered and said to her, "Martha, Martha, you are worried and troubled about many things. But one thing is needed, and Mary has chosen that good part, which will not be taken away from her."

2. **Psalm 138:8** — The Lord will perfect that which concerns me; Your mercy O Lord, endures forever; Do not forsake the works of Your hands.

3. **Philemon 1:6** — That the sharing of your faith may become effective by the acknowledgment of every good thing which is in you in Christ Jesus.

SYNOPSIS

The story of Martha is a cautionary example of what can happen when we become overwhelmed with the busyness of life and neglect our time with Jesus. Although Martha was gifted in hospitality and serving others, she became distracted from the most important thing she needed to do — and that was sitting at the feet of the Master. When Jesus corrected her, He was also giving her an invitation to receive something special from Him that would balance out her life and bring peace to her anxious heart.

The emphasis of this lesson:

At the end of our spiritual race, we will one day experience the great wonder of seeing Jesus face to face. What a joyful moment to look forward to in Heaven! Although we may not see Jesus today with our physical eyes, we can still experience His presence as we walk with Him on this earth. While we continue to run our race, it's vital to our spiritual health to spend time every day listening to the Holy Spirit and fellowshipping with Him. When we respond to His invitation, we receive the revelation He desired to give us so that we can finish our course with joy!

Experiencing Jesus as You Run Your Race

The Bible tells us that as we run our race, we are to look unto Jesus who is the Author and Finisher of our faith. Can you imagine what it will be like to see Jesus face to face once we have crossed over into eternity? What an experience that will be to behold Him in all His glory and splendor!

While we may not see Jesus with our physical eyes on this earth, we can still experience His presence as we walk with Him. In fact, Jesus wants us to experience Him, to hear Him, and to have fellowship with Him every day. Although we can't physically touch Jesus until we reach Heaven, we can know Him through His Word and the Holy Spirit.

Because the Holy Spirit lives on the inside of us, He will lead us and guide us into all truth. He will teach us, comfort us, and glorify Jesus. When the Holy Spirit's presence comes, He brings healing, miracles, peace, and joy. He brings calmness to our hearts because He glorifies Jesus. Isn't that magnificent?

It's so important to spend time with the Holy Spirit and experience Him for all He is, especially as we enter the last days. We need the power and the peace of God to hold us steady through tumultuous times! Thankfully, the Holy Spirit lives inside us always — even in the most difficult situations!

Before Jesus left the earth, He told His disciples that it was better for them if He left so that the Holy Spirit could come. Today, we understand the power and presence of the Holy Spirit living inside us and how wonderful it is to have fellowship with Him everywhere we go, every single day.

The Bible says that the Holy Spirit will take what belongs to Jesus and declare it to us (*see* John 16:14). He gives us revelation of who Jesus is and all that He has given to us through His death and resurrection. He testifies of the character and nature of Jesus, and He glorifies Him when He moves and demonstrates Himself.

Martha's Personal Experience With Jesus

When Jesus lived on this earth, many people experienced Him in a physical, tangible way. They didn't have the Holy Spirit living inside them, but they could know Jesus and see the heart of God by being around Him and spending time with Him. Those who came to Jesus in faith and recognized Him as the Son of God received miracles, healing, peace, and love as He ministered to them. They also received revelation, instruction, and correction as Jesus taught them the ways of the Kingdom.

One particular woman named Martha had a rather unusual experience with Jesus as He was ministering in her house one day. She, her sister Mary, and her brother Lazarus were friends of Jesus, and they often welcomed Him into their home for times of fellowship and ministry. Luke recorded this event and gave insight into Martha's character and how she responded to the Master's visit.

Luke 10:38 says, "Now it happened as they went that He entered a certain village; and a certain woman named Martha welcomed Him into her house." When this passage is taught, people often focus their attention on Martha's anxiousness in this story. However, Martha's character should not be deemed as completely negative — in fact, she was actually very hospitable! She was the one who welcomed Jesus into her home, which reveals the gift of hospitality that was present within her.

If you've ever been privileged enough to be invited into a home by someone who has the gift of hospitality, you know it's an amazing gift. When you come into their house, you feel so welcome and special. They do everything just to serve you and make you feel comfortable during your visit.

This gift of hospitality is precious, and it's something Martha possessed. When guests like Jesus came into her home, she was concerned about their comfort and well-being. She was completely engaged in the act of serving because that was the gift operating in her!

Now, during this particular visit recorded in Luke 10, Martha wasn't ignoring Jesus by not taking any time to listen to Him. In fact, verse 39 says, "And she had a sister called Mary, who *also* sat at Jesus' feet and heard His word." Because this verse uses the word "also," we understand there was a time during Jesus' visit when Martha was sitting down at His feet just like Mary.

However, over the course of the visit, something happened that distracted Mary and caused her to get up from where she was seated and stop listening to the words of the Master. Verse 40 says, "But Martha was distracted with much serving, and she approached Him and said, 'Lord, do You not care that my sister has left me to serve alone? Therefore, tell her to help me."

From this passage, we can see that Martha was overwhelmed with the task of serving and taking care of the guests that were in her home. She was anxious, weighed down, and distracted. This *carefulness* (being full of care) caused her to pull away from the opportunity to receive ministry from Jesus.

Perhaps you can relate to Martha's personality and experience. In using your gift to serve others, have you ever lost sight of your personal fellowship with Jesus? It can be easy to do if you're not intentional! However, it's important to regularly examine your heart. If there are things that are clogging your relationship with the Lord or distracting you from spending daily time with Him, then it would be good for you to pull back from doing so many external things so you can hear from Jesus. Many natural things in life can wait for those few extra moments of spending time with the Lord.

Because Martha was getting so worked up and anxious about serving, Jesus said to her, "Martha, Martha, you are worried and troubled about many things. But one thing is needed, and Mary has chosen that good part, which shall not be taken away from her." (Luke 10:41,42). In essence, Jesus was saying, "Martha, I want you to sit down here with Mary just for a minute. The fig casserole will be okay. What I have to speak to you is so much more valuable than the natural things you are concerned with at the moment."

Interestingly enough, the phrase "one thing is needed" used in verse 42 means *a deficit*. In other words, Jesus was telling Martha that there was *a deficit in her life*, and she needed to come to Him to receive the balance that was missing. He wasn't instructing her not to serve but rather to prioritize her relationship with Him.

Just like Martha, we need God's presence in our daily lives. When we don't spend adequate time fellowshipping with Jesus, there is something missing in our day. We begin to have a deficit, and the only remedy to balance out our lives is personal time with Him.

As we go through our day, we may encounter problems that test our patience or steal our joy. By spending time with Jesus, we will have an ample supply of patience and joy to confront those challenging situations. However, if we skip our time with Him, we won't have the supernatural supply necessary that comes from spending time in the presence of the Master to overcome those daily challenges.

We need to recognize the power of the Holy Spirit living inside us. By spending time with Him every day, we have an opportunity to receive from Him and grow in His likeness. When we're tempted to react to people or circumstances in the flesh, we can respond to them from the well of salvation that is in us simply because we've spent time drinking from the Water of Life!

The Revelation of the Invitation

What Jesus spoke to Martha in Luke 10 is what He is speaking to us today — He is inviting us to spend time in His presence. Every day He is inviting us to draw nearer to Him and to receive His peace, His wisdom,

His joy, His patience, and His power. Of course, we can ignore His invitation, but we would be missing out on what He desires to impart to us. It is only by spending time with Him that our deficit can be filled.

God has given us a special promise in Psalm 138:8 that says, "The Lord will perfect that which concerns me...." We may encounter difficulties and even horrible situations from time to time, but God can see us through every trial if we will stay close to Him. Instead of being overwhelmed by problems, we can overcome them through the power of the Holy Spirit.

We have something in us that Martha didn't have — we have the Holy Spirit living inside us. Whenever we become worried or agitated about something, He is inviting us to come and listen to Him. He'll speak up from the inside and say, "Listen. Calm down. The frustration you're facing is not worth screaming and yelling about. Don't lose your peace. Just come to Me, and I will give you the wisdom, peace, and patience you need to handle this issue."

No matter what situations we may be facing, it's important for us to slow down enough to recognize that still, small voice inside us. Instead of worrying about things, we can quiet our minds and mouths just for a moment and listen to the Holy Spirit. He is inviting us to come, and it's our choice whether or not we will respond to that invitation.

By choosing the "one needful thing" that Mary chose in Luke 10, we will be fully satisfied! The revelation the Holy Spirit gives us in our times of seeking Him will not be taken away from us. It's needful that we hear from Him and obey His voice. His words are precious to us, and what we have received from Him is invaluable.

The Lord is not against you doing things that are useful and necessary in this natural life. He is not against a busy mother who is cleaning her house, taking care of her children, or supporting her husband. He's not against a busy businesswoman or a dedicated student. All of our responsibilities in life take time and focus. But God does want us to get alone with Him, so He can pour Himself into us in the way He did with Mary that day. He is inviting every one of us — just like He invited Martha — to take His yoke upon us and to do things with His grace and power.

The Bible instructs us in Philemon 1:6 to acknowledge every good thing within us by Christ Jesus. We need to take notice and pay attention to the wonderful things inside us by the Holy Spirit. The peace inside us is a weapon against anxiety, worry, and fear. We have this treasure inside us to defeat the enemy. All that God has deposited in our spirits can overcome the pressure and disturbance coming from this world. Isn't that magnificent?

So as we are running our race, we don't have to become fatigued or overwhelmed by challenges that come against us. By responding to Jesus' invitation to draw near to Him and listen to His voice, we can receive the revelation, strength, peace, and wisdom necessary to keep running the race set before us. By choosing that one needful thing — spending time with Jesus — we can experience His presence every single day!

STUDY QUESTIONS

**Be diligent to present yourself approved to God, a worker
who does not need to be ashamed, rightly dividing the word of truth.
— 2 Timothy 2:15**

1. In Luke 10, we read the story of two sisters, Mary and Martha, and the very different responses they had when presented with the opportunity to spend time with Jesus. Which sister are you more like?

2. Psalm 138:8 says, "The Lord will perfect that which concerns me; Your mercy O Lord, endures forever; Do not forsake the works of Your hands." How does this verse encourage you today?

3. Philemon 1:6 says, "That the sharing of your faith may become effective by the acknowledgment of every good thing which is in you in Christ Jesus." What good thing has God deposited in you that you have been acknowledging recently?

PRACTICAL APPLICATION

**But be doers of the word,
and not hearers only, deceiving yourselves.
— James 1:22**

Don't allow anything to distract you from spending time with Jesus.

1. What things in life have a tendency to distract you from spending time with Jesus? What can you do to overcome these distractions so you can hear properly from the Lord?

2. Are you facing a situation that is testing your patience? What is the Holy Spirit speaking to your heart about how to deal with that

situation, so you are no longer overwhelmed by it but are walking in the fruit of the spirit instead?

What gifts has God blessed you with in your life? Do you sometimes get so busy doing the natural things with your gifts that you forget to spend time with Jesus?

STUDY QUESTIONS

Be diligent to present yourself approved to God, a worker
who does not need to be ashamed, rightly dividing the word of truth.
— 2 Timothy 2:15

1. Second Corinthians 3:18 says, "But we all, with unveiled face, beholding as in a mirror the glory of the Lord, are being transformed into the same image from glory to glory, just as by the Spirit of the Lord." Reading the Bible is critical to our spiritual growth and transformation. What other passages of scripture do you know that admonish us to meditate on or study God's Word? What are the benefits of studying the Bible?

2. In this series, we examined the lives of four people in the Old Testament who were changed by the presence of God. What other people from the Bible can you think of who were transformed by the power of God?

3. Of all four examples we have studied in this series, which one impacted you the most? Which one do you relate to the most and why?

PRACTICAL APPLICATION

But be doers of the word,
and not hearers only, deceiving yourselves.
— James 1:22

1. Hebrews 11 is often referred to as the Hall of Faith. Take some time today to study that chapter. What other Bible characters are mentioned in this chapter that exemplify a life of faith? If you're not familiar with some of their stories, make it a point to read the passages of scripture where their lives are mentioned.

2. In your Bible reading this week, what has the Lord been speaking to you about specifically? How are you being changed from glory to glory by spending time in His Word?

3. As we learned in our study, God can change our identity, give us a new assignment, and give us the strength to fulfill that assignment whenever we encounter the presence of God. In what ways has God changed your identity? What new assignment has He given you? How have you been strengthened or empowered to accomplish His plan for your life?

Notes

_____
_____
_____
_____
_____
_____
_____
_____
_____
_____
_____
_____
_____
_____
_____
_____
_____
_____
_____
_____
_____
_____
_____
_____
_____
_____
_____
_____
_____
_____

Notes

Notes

CLAIM YOUR FREE RESOURCE!

As a way of introducing you further to the teaching ministry of Rick Renner, we would like to send you free of charge his teaching CD, "How To Receive a Miraculous Touch From God."

How To Receive a Miraculous Touch From God
Rick Renner

CD36

RENNER

In His earthly ministry, Jesus commonly healed *all* who were sick of *all* their diseases. In this profound message, learn about the manifold dimensions of Christ's wisdom, goodness, power, and love toward all humanity who came to Him in faith with their needs.

☑ **YES, I want to receive Rick Renner's monthly teaching letter!**

Simply scan the QR code to claim this resource or go to: **renner.org/claim-your-free-offer**

Connect
WITH US!

R renner.org

- **f** facebook.com/rickrenner • facebook.com/rennerdenise
- **▶** youtube.com/rennerministries • youtube.com/deniserenner
- **⊙** instagram.com/rickrenner • instagram.com/rennerministries_ instagram.com/rennerdenise

www.ingramcontent.com/pod-product-compliance
Lightning Source LLC
Chambersburg PA
CBHW051050030426
42339CB00006B/283